low fat

This is a Star Fire book
First Published in 2005

06 08 09 07 05

1 3 5 7 9 10 8 6 4 2

Star Fire is part of The Foundry Creative Media Company Limited
Crabtree Hall, Crabtree Lane, Fulham, London, SW6 6TY
Please visit the our website: *www.star-fire.co.uk*

Please visit our cookery website: *www.practicalrecipes.com*

Copyright © The Foundry 2005

ISBN: 1-904041-31-0

The CIP record for this book is available from the British Library

Printed in China

ACKNOWLEDGEMENTS

Authors: Catherine Atkinson, Juliet Barker, Liz Martin,
Gina Steer, Carol Tennant, Mari Mereid Williams,
Elizabeth Wolf-Cohen, Simone Wright

Editorial Consultant: Gina Steer
Project Editor: Sarah Goulding

Editors: Karen Fitzpatrick, Vicky Garrard, Julia Rolf
Photography: Colin Bowling and Paul Forrester

Home Economists and Stylists: Jacqueline Bellefontaine,
Mandy Phipps, Vicki Smallwood and Penny Stephens

Design Team: Lucy Bradbury and Chris Herbert

All props supplied by Barbara Stewart at Surfaces

NOTE

Recipes using uncooked eggs should be avoided by infants, the
elderly, pregnant women and anyone suffering from an illness.

simple, straightforward recipes

low fat

Contents

Store Cupboard Essentials
Low Fat Ingredients for a Healthy Lifestyle

Low fat cooking has often been associated with the stigma that reducing fat reduces flavour. This simply is not the case, which is great news for those choosing a lower-fat diet.

The store cupboard is a good place to start when cooking low fat meals. It is always a good idea, especially when following a low fat diet, to have some well-thought-out basics in the cupboard – foods that are high on flavour and low in fat.

As store cupboard ingredients keep reasonably well, it really is worth making a trip to a good speciality grocery shop.

If the grocers or local supermarket only carries a limited choice of products, do not despair. The Internet now offers freedom to the food shopaholics amongst us. There are some fantastic food sites (both local and international) where food can be purchased and delivery arranged online.

When thinking about essentials, think of flavour, something that is going to add to a dish without increasing its fat content. It is worth spending a little bit more money on these products to make flavoursome dishes that will help stop the urge to snack on fatty foods.

COUSCOUS A precooked wheat semolina. Traditional couscous needs to be steamed and is available from health food stores. This type of couscous contains more nutrients than the instant variety which just needs to be covered with boiling water.

DRIED FRUIT The ready-to-eat variety are particularly good as they are plump, juicy and do not need to be soaked. They are fantastic when puréed into a compote, added to water and heated to make a pie filling and when added to stuffing mixtures. They are also good cooked with meats, rice or couscous.

FLOURS A useful addition (particularly cornflour) which can be used to thicken sauces. While not strictly a flour, cornmeal is a very versatile low fat ingredient, which can be used when making dumplings and gnocchi.

NOODLES Noodles are also very useful and can accompany any Far Eastern dish. They are low fat and also available in the wholewheat variety. Rice noodles are available for those who have gluten-free diets and, like pasta noodles, provide slow-release energy to the body.

PASTA Whether fresh or dried, pasta is a versatile ingredient which provides the body with slow-release energy. It comes in many different sizes and shapes; from the tiny tubettini to the larger cannelloni and lasagne sheets.

BARLEY A cereal low in gluten, which is chiefly used in soups and stews.

PULSES High in nutritional value and a good source

of slow-release carbohydrate as well as protein. They come in two forms; either dried (in which case they generally need to be soaked overnight and then cooked before use – it is important to follow the instructions on the back of the packet), or canned. If buying canned pulses, try to buy the variety in water with no added salt or sugar. These simply need to be drained and rinsed before being added to a dish.

Kidney borlotti, cannellini, butter and flageolet beans, split peas and lentils, all make tasty additions to any dish. Baked beans are a favourite with everyone and many shops now stock the organic variety, which have no added salt or sugar but are sweetened with fruit juice instead.

When boiling previously dried pulses, remember that salt should not be added as this will make the skins tough and inedible. Puy lentils are a smaller variety of lentil. They often have mottled skins and are good for cooking in slow dishes as they hold their shape and firm texture particularly well.

RICE Basmati and Thai fragrant rice are well suited to Thai and Indian curries as the fine grains absorb the sauce and their delicate creaminess balances the pungency of the spices. Arborio is only one type of risotto rice. Many are available depending on whether the risotto is meant to accompany meat, fish or vegetable dishes. When cooked, rice swells to create a substantial low fat dish. Easy-cook American rice, both plain and wholegrain, is great for casseroles and for stuffing meat, fish and vegetables as it holds its shape and firmness. Pudding rice can be used in a variety of ways to create an irresistible dessert.

STOCK AND SAUCE BASES Good quality stock is a must in low fat cooking as it provides a good flavour base for many dishes. Many supermarkets now carry a variety of fresh and organic stocks. There is also a fairly large range of dried stock, perhaps the best being bouillon, a high-quality form of stock (available in powder or liquid form) which can be added to any dish whether it be a sauce, casserole, pie or soup.

A good quality passata sauce or canned plum tomatoes can act as the foundation for any sauce, as can a good quality green or red pesto. Other handy store cupboard additions include tapenade, mustard and anchovies. These ingredients have very distinctive tastes and are particularly flavoursome. Roasted red pepper sauce and sundried tomato purée, which tends to be sweeter and more intensely flavoured than regular tomato purée, are also very useful.

Using herbs when cooking at home should reduce the temptation to buy ready-made sauces. Often these types of sauces contain large amounts of sugar and additives.

Eastern flavours offer a lot of scope where low fat cooking is concerned. Flavourings such as fish sauce, soy sauce, red and green curry paste and Chinese rice wine all offer mouthwatering low fat flavours to any dish.

Aubergine & Yogurt Dip

Ingredients

Makes 600 ml/ 1 pint

2 x 225 g/8 oz
   aubergines
1 tbsp light olive oil
1 tbsp lemon juice
2 garlic cloves, peeled
   and crushed
190 g jar pimentos,
   drained
150 ml/¼ pint low fat
   natural yogurt
salt and freshly ground
   black pepper
25 g/1 oz black olives,
   pitted and chopped
225 g/8 oz
   cauliflower florets
225 g/8 oz
   broccoli florets
125 g/4 oz carrots,
   peeled and cut into
   5 cm/2 inch strips

CHEF'S TIP
Following the Middle Eastern style of this dish, why not also serve pieces of warmed, unleavened bread such as naan or pitta with the dip.

1 Preheat the oven to 200°C/400°F/Gas Mark 6. Pierce the skin of the aubergines with a fork and place on a baking tray. Cook for 40 minutes or until very soft.

2 Cool the aubergines, then cut in half, and scoop out the flesh and tip into a bowl.

3 Mash the aubergine with the olive oil, lemon juice and garlic until smooth or blend for a few seconds in a food processor.

4 Chop the pimentos into small cubes and add to the aubergine mixture.

5 When blended add the yogurt. Stir well and season to taste with salt and pepper.

6 Add the chopped olives and leave in the refrigerator to chill for at least 30 minutes.

7 Place the cauliflower and broccoli florets and carrot strips into a pan and cover with boiling water. Simmer for 2 minutes, then rinse in cold water. Drain and serve as crudités to accompany the dip.

Bulghur Wheat Salad with Minty Lemon Dressing

Ingredients

Serves 4

125 g/4 oz
  bulghur wheat
10 cm/4 inch
  piece cucumber
2 shallots, peeled
125 g/4 oz baby
  sweetcorn
3 ripe but
  firm tomatoes

For the dressing:

grated rind of 1 lemon
3 tbsp lemon juice
3 tbsp freshly
  chopped mint
2 tbsp freshly
  chopped parsley
1–2 tsp clear honey
2 tbsp sunflower oil
salt and freshly ground
  black pepper

1 Place the bulghur wheat in a saucepan and cover with boiling water.

2 Simmer for about 10 minutes, then drain thoroughly and turn into a serving bowl.

3 Cut the cucumber into small dice, chop the shallots finely and reserve. Steam the sweetcorn over a pan of boiling water for 10 minutes or until tender. Drain and slice into thick chunks.

4 Cut a cross on the top of each tomato and place in boiling water until their skins start to peel away.

5 Remove the skins and the seeds and cut the tomatoes into small dice.

6 Make the dressing by briskly whisking all the ingredients in a small bowl until mixed well.

7 When the bulghur wheat has cooled a little, add all the prepared vegetables and stir in the dressing. Season to taste with salt and pepper and serve.

Chicken & Summer Vegetable Risotto

Ingredients
Serves 4

1 litre/1¾ pint chicken
   or vegetable stock
225 g/8 oz baby
   asparagus spears
125 g/4 oz French beans
15 g/½ oz butter
1 small onion, peeled
   and finely chopped
150 ml/¼ pint dry
   white wine
275 g/10 oz arborio rice
pinch of
   saffron strands
75 g/3 oz frozen
   peas, thawed
225 g/8 oz cooked
   chicken, skinned
   and diced
juice of ½ lemon
salt and freshly ground
   black pepper
25 g/1 oz
   Parmesan, shaved

1 Bring the stock to the boil in a large saucepan. Trim the asparagus and cut into 4 cm/1½ inch lengths. Blanch the asparagus in the stock for 1–2 minutes or until tender, then remove with a slotted spoon and reserve.

2 Halve the green beans and cook in the boiling stock for 4 minutes. Remove and reserve. Turn down the heat and keep the stock barely simmering.

3 Melt the butter in a heavy-based saucepan. Add the onion and cook gently for about 5 minutes.

4 Pour the wine into the pan and boil rapidly until the liquid has almost reduced. Add the rice and cook, stirring for 1 minute until the grains are coated and look translucent.

5 Add the saffron and a ladle of the stock. Simmer, stirring all the time, until the stock has absorbed. Continue adding the stock, a ladle at a time, until it has all been absorbed.

6 After 15 minutes the risotto should be creamy with a slight bite to it. If not add a little more stock and cook for a few more minutes, or until it is of the correct texture and consistency.

7 Add the peas, reserved vegetables, chicken and lemon juice. Season to taste with salt and pepper and cook for 3-4 minutes or until the chicken is thoroughly heated and piping hot. Serve with parmesan shavings

Chicken Cacciatore

Ingredients
Serves 4

4 chicken leg portions
1 tbsp olive oil
1 red onion, peeled
    and cut into very
    thin wedges
1 garlic clove, peeled
    and crushed
sprig of fresh thyme
sprig of fresh rosemary
150 ml/¼ pint dry
    white wine
200 ml/7 fl oz
    chicken stock
400 g can chopped
    tomatoes
40 g/1½ oz black
    olives, pitted
15 g/½ oz capers, drained
salt and freshly ground
    black pepper
freshly cooked
    fettuccine, linguine
    or pasta shells

1 Skin the chicken portions and cut each one into two pieces to make four thighs and four drumsticks.

2 Heat 2 teaspoons of the oil in a flameproof casserole dish and cook the chicken for 2–3 minutes on each side until lightly browned. Remove the chicken from the pan and reserve.

3 Add the remaining 1 teaspoon of oil to the juices in the pan.

4 Add the red onion to the pan and gently cook for 5 minutes, stirring occasionally.

5 Add the garlic and cook for a further 5 minutes until soft and beginning to brown. Return the chicken to the pan.

6 Add the herbs, then pour in the wine and let it bubble for 1–2 minutes.

7 Add the stock and tomatoes, cover and gently simmer for 15 minutes.

8 Stir in the olives and capers. Cook uncovered for a further 5 minutes or until the chicken is cooked and the sauce thickened. Remove the herbs and season to taste with salt and pepper.

9 Place the chicken on a bed of pasta, allowing one thigh and one drumstick per person. Spoon over the sauce and serve.

Chicken with Roasted Fennel & Citrus Rice

Ingredients
Serves 4

2 tsp fennel seeds
1 tbsp freshly
   chopped oregano
1 garlic clove, peeled
   and crushed
salt and freshly ground
   black pepper
4 chicken quarters,
   about 175 g/6 oz each
½ lemon, finely sliced
1 fennel bulb, trimmed
2 tsp olive oil
4 plum tomatoes
25 g/1 oz stoned
   green olives

For the
citrus rice:

225 g/8 oz long-
   grain rice
finely grated rind and
   juice of ½ lemon
150 ml/¼ pint
   orange juice
450 ml/¾ pint
   boiling chicken or
   vegetable stock

To garnish:

fennel fronds
orange slices

1 Preheat the oven to 200°C/400°F/Gas Mark 6. Lightly crush the fennel seeds and mix with oregano, garlic, salt and pepper. Place between the skin and flesh of the chicken breasts, careful not to tear the skin. Arrange the lemon slices on top of the chicken.

2 Cut the fennel into eight wedges. Place on baking tray with the chicken. Lightly brush the fennel with the oil. Cook the chicken and fennel on the top shelf of the preheated oven for 10 minutes.

3 Meanwhile, put the rice in a 2.3 litre/4 pint ovenproof dish. Stir in the lemon rind and juice, orange juice and stock. Cover with a lid and put on the middle shelf of the oven.

4 Reduce the oven temperature to 180°C/350°F/Gas Mark 4. Cook the chicken for a further 40 minutes, turning the fennel wedges and lemon slices once. Deseed and chop the tomatoes. Add to the tray and cook for 5–10 minutes. Remove from the oven.

5 When cooled slightly, remove the chicken skin and discard. Fluff the rice, scatter olives over the dish. Garnish with fennel fronds, orange slices and serve.

Crispy Baked Potatoes with Serrano Ham

Ingredients
Serves 4

4 large baking potatoes
4 tsp half-fat
   crème fraîche
salt and freshly ground
   black pepper
50 g/2 oz lean Serrano
   ham or prosciutto,
   with fat removed
50 g/2 oz cooked baby
   broad beans
50 g/2 oz cooked
   carrots, diced
50 g/2 oz cooked peas
50 g/2 oz low fat hard
   cheese such as Edam
   or Cheddar, grated
fresh green salad,
   to serve

1 Preheat the oven to 200°C/400°F/Gas Mark 6. Scrub the potatoes dry. Prick with a fork and place on a baking sheet. Cook for 1–1½ hours or until tender when squeezed. Use oven gloves or a kitchen towel to pick up the potatoes as they will be very hot.

2 Cut the potatoes in half horizontally and scoop out all the flesh into a bowl.

3 Spoon the crème fraîche into the bowl and mix thoroughly with the potatoes. Season to taste with a little salt and pepper.

4 Cut the ham into strips and carefully stir into the potato mixture with the broad beans, carrots and peas.

5 Pile the mixture back into the eight potato shells and sprinkle a little grated cheese on the top.

6 Place under a hot grill and cook until golden and heated through. Serve immediately with a fresh green salad.

CHEF'S TIP
Produced in Spain, Serrano ham has a sweet, succulent taste and is traditionally carved along the grain. If you cannot find Serrano ham, you can use prosciutto instead.

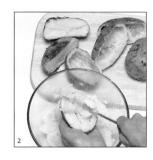

Curly Endive & Seafood Salad

Ingredients
Serves 4

1 head of curly
  endive lettuce
2 green peppers
12.5 cm/5 inch piece
  of cucumber
125 g/4 oz squid,
  cleaned and cut
  into thin rings
225 g/8 oz baby
  asparagus spears
125 g/4 oz smoked
  salmon slices, cut
  into wide strips
175 g/6 oz fresh
  cooked mussels
  in their shells

For the lemon dressing:

2 tbsp sunflower oil
1 tbsp white
  wine vinegar
5 tbsp fresh
  lemon juice
1–2 tsp caster sugar
1 tsp mild whole-
  grain mustard
salt and freshly ground
  black pepper

To garnish:

slices of lemon
sprigs of
  fresh coriander

1 Rinse and tear the endive into small pieces and arrange on a serving platter.

2 Remove the seeds from the peppers and cut the peppers and the cucumber into small dice. Sprinkle over the endive.

3 Bring a saucepan of water to the boil and add the squid rings. Bring the pan up to the boil again, then switch off the heat and leave it to stand for 5 minutes. Then drain and rinse thoroughly in cold water.

4 Cook the asparagus in boiling water for 5 minutes or until tender but just crisp. Arrange with the squid, smoked salmon and mussels on top of the salad.

5 To make the lemon dressing, put all the ingredients into a screw-topped jar or into a small bowl and mix thoroughly until the ingredients are combined.

6 Spoon 3 tablespoons of the dressing over the salad and serve the remainder in a small jug. Garnish the salad with slices of lemon and sprigs of coriander and serve.

Duck with Berry Sauce

Ingredients
Serves 4

4 x 175 g/6 oz boneless
   duck breasts
salt and freshly ground
   black pepper
1 tsp sunflower oil

For the sauce:

juice of 1 orange
1 bay leaf
3 tbsp redcurrant jelly
150 g/5 oz fresh or
   frozen mixed berries
2 tbsp dried cranberries
   or cherries
½ tsp soft light
   brown sugar
1 tbsp balsamic vinegar
1 tsp freshly
   chopped mint
sprigs of fresh mint,
   to garnish

To serve:

freshly cooked potatoes
freshly cooked
   green beans

CHEF'S TIP
Scald the duck by pouring
boiling water over it to
drain off excess fat and
make the skin extra crispy.

1 Remove the skins from the duck breasts and season with a little salt and pepper. Brush a griddle pan with the oil, then heat on the stove until smoking hot.

2 Place the duck, skinned-side down in the pan. Cook over a medium-high heat for 5 minutes, or until well browned. Turn the duck and cook for 2 minutes. Lower the heat and cook for a further 5–8 minutes, or until cooked, but still slightly pink in the centre. Remove from the pan and keep warm.

3 While the duck is cooking, make the sauce. Put the orange juice, bay leaf, redcurrant jelly, fresh or frozen and dried berries and sugar in a small griddle pan. Add any juices left in the griddle pan to the small pan. Slowly bring to the boil, lower the heat and simmer uncovered for 4–5 minutes, until the fruit is soft.

4 Remove the bay leaf. Stir in the vinegar and chopped mint and season to taste with salt and pepper.

5 Slice the duck breasts on the diagonal and arrange on serving plates. Spoon over the berry sauce and garnish with sprigs of fresh mint. Serve immediately with the potatoes and green beans.

Gingered Cod Steaks

Ingredients

Serves 4

2.5 cm /1 inch
   piece fresh root
   ginger, peeled
4 spring onions
2 tsp freshly
   chopped parsley
1 tbsp soft brown sugar
4 x 175 g /6 oz thick
   cod steaks
salt and freshly ground
   black pepper
25 g/1 oz half-fat butter
freshly cooked
   vegetables, to serve

1 Preheat the grill and line the grill rack with a layer of tinfoil. Coarsely grate the piece of ginger. Trim the spring onions and cut into thin strips.

2 Mix the spring onions, ginger, chopped parsley and sugar. Add 1 tablespoon of water.

3 Wipe the fish steaks. Season to taste with salt and pepper. Place on to four separate 20.5 x 20.5 cm/8 x 8 inch tinfoil squares.

4 Carefully spoon the spring onions and ginger mixture over the fish.

5 Cut the butter into small cubes and place over the fish.

6 Loosely fold the foil over the steaks to enclose the fish and to make a parcel.

7 Place under the preheated grill and cook for 10–12 minutes or until cooked and the flesh has turned opaque.

8 Place the fish parcels on individual serving plates. Serve immediately with the freshly cooked vegetables.

CHEF'S TIP
If you prefer a more gentle ginger flavour, slice the ginger instead of grating and remove the pieces before serving.

Guinea Fowl with Calvados & Apples

Ingredients
Serves 4

4 guinea fowl
   supremes, each
   about 150 g/5 oz,
   skinned
1 tbsp plain flour
1 tbsp sunflower oil
1 onion, peeled and
   finely sliced
1 garlic clove, peeled
   and crushed
1 tsp freshly
   chopped thyme
150 ml/¼ pint dry cider
salt and freshly ground
   black pepper
3 tbsp Calvados brandy
sprigs of fresh thyme,
   to garnish

Caramelised apples:

15 g/½ oz unsalted
   butter
2 red-skinned eating
   apples, quartered,
   cored and sliced
1 tsp caster sugar

1 Lightly dust the guinea fowl supremes with the flour. Heat 2 teaspoons of the oil in a large non-stick frying pan and cook the supremes for 2–3 minutes on each side until browned. Remove from the pan and reserve.

2 Heat the remaining teaspoon of oil in the pan and add the onion and garlic. Cook over a medium heat for 10 minutes, stirring occasionally until soft and just beginning to colour.

3 Stir in the chopped thyme and cider. Return the guinea fowl to the pan, season with salt and pepper and bring to a very gentle simmer. Cover and cook over a low heat for 15–20 minutes or until the guinea fowl is tender.

4 Remove the guinea fowl and keep warm. Turn up the heat and boil the sauce until thickened and reduced by half.

5 Meanwhile, prepare the caramelised apples. Melt the butter in a small non-stick pan, add the apple slices in a single layer and sprinkle with the sugar. Cook until the apples are tender and beginning to caramelise, turning once.

6 Put the Calvados in a metal ladle or small saucepan and gently heat until warm. Carefully set alight with a match, let the flames die down, then stir into the sauce. Pour sauce over the guinea fowl to serve, and garnish with the apples.

Hoisin Chicken Pancakes

Ingredients
Serves 4

3 tbsp hoisin sauce
1 garlic clove, peeled
   and crushed
2.5 cm/1 inch piece root
   ginger, peeled and
   finely grated
1 tbsp soy sauce
1 tsp sesame oil
salt and freshly ground
   black pepper
4 skinless
   chicken thighs
½ cucumber,
   peeled (optional)
12 bought
   Chinese pancakes
6 spring onions,
   trimmed and cut
   lengthways into
   fine shreds
sweet chilli dipping
   sauce, to serve

1 Preheat the oven to 190°C/375°F/Gas Mark 5. In a non-metallic bowl, mix the hoisin sauce with the garlic, ginger, soy sauce, sesame oil and seasoning.

2 Add the chicken thighs and turn to coat in the mixture. Cover loosely and leave in the refrigerator to marinate for 3–4 hours, turning the chicken from time to time.

3 Remove the chicken from the marinade and place in a roasting tin. Reserve the marinade. Bake in the preheated oven for 30 minutes, basting occasionally with the marinade.

4 Cut the cucumber in half lengthways and remove the seeds by running a teaspoon down the middle to scoop them out. Cut into thin batons.

5 Place the pancakes in a steamer to warm or heat according to packet instructions. Thinly slice the hot chicken and arrange on a plate with the shredded spring onions, cucumber and pancakes.

6 Place a spoonful of the chicken in the middle of each warmed pancake and top with pieces of cucumber, spring onion, and a little dipping sauce. Roll up and serve immediately.

Honey & Ginger Prawns

Ingredients
Serves 4

1 carrot
50 g/2 oz
   bamboo shoots
4 spring onions
1 tbsp clear honey
1 tbsp tomato ketchup
1 tsp soy sauce
2.5 cm/1 inch piece
   of fresh root
   ginger, peeled
   and finely grated
1 garlic clove, peeled
   and crushed
1 tbsp lime juice
175 g/6 oz peeled
   prawns, thawed
   if frozen
2 heads little gem
   lettuce leaves
2 tbsp freshly
   chopped coriander
salt and freshly ground
   black pepper

To garnish:

fresh coriander sprigs
lime slices

1 Cut the carrot into matchstick-size pieces, roughly chop the bamboo shoots and finely slice the spring onions.

2 Combine the bamboo shoots with the carrot matchsticks and spring onions.

3 In a wok or large frying pan gently heat the honey, tomato ketchup, soy sauce, ginger, garlic and lime juice with 3 tablespoons of water. Bring to the boil.

4 Add the carrot mixture and stir-fry for 2–3 minutes until the vegetables are hot.

5 Add the prawns and continue to stir-fry for 2 minutes.

6 Remove the wok or frying pan from the heat and reserve until cooled slightly.

7 Divide the little gem lettuce into leaves and rinse lightly.

8 Stir the chopped coriander into the prawn mixture and season to taste with salt and pepper. Spoon into the lettuce leaves and serve immediately garnished with sprigs of fresh coriander and lime slices.

Hot Salsa-filled Sole

Ingredients
Serves 4

8 x 175 g/6 oz lemon
sole fillets, skinned
150 ml/¼ pint
orange juice
2 tbsp lemon juice

For the salsa:

1 small mango
8 cherry tomatoes,
quartered
1 small red onion,
peeled and
finely chopped
pinch of sugar
1 red chilli
2 tbsp rice vinegar
zest and juice of 1 lime
1 tbsp olive oil
sea salt and freshly
ground black pepper
2 tbsp freshly
chopped mint
lime wedges, to garnish
salad leaves, to serve

1 First make the salsa. Peel the mango and cut the flesh away from the stone. Chop finely and place in a small bowl. Add the cherry tomatoes to the mango together with the onion and sugar.

2 Cut the top off the chilli. Slit down the side and discard the seeds and the membrane (the skin to which the seeds are attached). Finely chop the chilli and add to the mango mixture with the vinegar, lime zest, juice and oil. Season to taste with salt and pepper. Mix thoroughly and leave to stand for 30 minutes to allow the flavours to develop.

3 Lay the fish fillets on a board skinned side up and pile the salsa on the tail end of the fillets. Fold the fillets in half, season and place in a large shallow frying pan. Pour over the orange and lemon juice.

4 Bring to a gentle boil, then reduce the heat to a simmer. Cover and cook on a low heat for 7–10 minutes, adding a little water if the liquid is evaporating. Remove the cover, add the mint and cook uncovered for a further 3 minutes. Garnish with lime wedges and serve immediately with the salad.

CHEF'S TIP
To temper the hotness of the salsa, add 1 or 2 teaspoons of warmed honey.

Huevos Rancheros

Ingredients
Serves 4

2 tbsp olive oil
1 large onion, peeled
    and finely chopped
1 red pepper, deseeded
    and finely chopped
2 garlic cloves, peeled
    and finely chopped
2–4 green chillies,
    deseeded and
    finely chopped
1 tsp ground cumin
1 tsp chilli powder
2 tsp ground coriander
2 tbsp freshly
    chopped coriander
700 g/1½ lb ripe plum
    tomatoes, peeled,
    deseeded and
    roughly chopped
¼ tsp sugar
8 small eggs
4–8 flour tortillas
salt and freshly ground
    black pepper
sprigs of fresh
    coriander, to garnish
refried beans, to serve
    (optional)

CHEF'S TIP
Flavoursome tomatoes can make a big difference to tomato dishes. It is worth using plum or victoria tomatoes as they have been left on the vine longer to ripen and have a better flavour.

1 Heat the oil in a large, heavy-based saucepan. Add the onion and pepper and cook over a medium heat for 10 minutes.

2 Add the garlic, chillies, ground cumin, chilli powder and chopped coriander and cook for a further minute.

3 Add the tomatoes and sugar. Stir well, cover and cook gently for 20 minutes. Uncover and cook for a further 20 minutes.

4 Lightly poach the eggs in a large frying pan, filled with gently simmering water. Drain well and keep warm.

5 Place the tortillas briefly under a preheated hot grill. Turning once, then remove from the grill when crisp.

6 Add the freshly chopped coriander to the tomato sauce and season to taste with salt and pepper.

7 To serve, arrange two tortillas on each serving plate, top with two eggs and spoon the sauce over. Garnish with sprigs of fresh coriander and serve immediately with warmed refried beans, if liked.

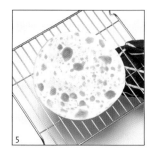

Mediterranean Feast

Ingredients
Serves 4

1 small iceberg lettuce
225 g/8 oz French beans
225 g/8 oz baby new
   potatoes, scrubbed
4 medium eggs
1 green pepper
1 medium onion, peeled
200 g can tuna in brine,
   drained and flaked
   into small pieces
50 g/2 oz low-fat hard
   cheese, such as Edam,
   cut into small cubes
8 ripe but firm cherry
   tomatoes, quartered
50 g/2 oz black pitted
   olives, halved
freshly chopped basil,
   to garnish

For the lime vinaigrette:

3 tbsp light olive oil
2 tbsp white
   wine vinegar
4 tbsp lime juice
grated rind of 1 lime
1 tsp Dijon mustard
1-2 tsp caster sugar
salt and freshly ground
   black pepper

CHEF'S TIP
Cans of tuna now include varieties such as yellow fin. Always choose tuna steaks over chunks.

1 Cut the lettuce into four and remove the hard core. Tear into bite-sized pieces and arrange on a large serving platter.

2 Cook the French beans in boiling salted water for 8 minutes and the potatoes for 10 minutes or until tender. Drain and rinse in cold water until cool, then cut both the beans and potatoes in half with a sharp knife.

3 Boil the eggs for 10 minutes, then rinse thoroughly under a cold running tap until cool. Remove the shells under water and cut each egg into four.

4 Remove the seeds from the pepper and cut into thin strips and finely chop the onion.

5 Arrange the beans, potatoes, eggs, peppers and onion on top of the lettuce. Add the tuna, cheese and tomatoes. Sprinkle over the olives and garnish with the basil.

6 To make the vinaigrette, place all the ingredients in a screw-topped jar and shake vigorously until everything is mixed thoroughly. Spoon 4 tablespoons over the top of the prepared salad and serve the remainder separately.

Mixed Salad with Anchovy Dressing & Ciabatta Croûtons

Ingredients
Serves 4

1 small head endive
1 small head chicory
1 fennel bulb
400 g can artichokes, drained and rinsed
½ cucumber
125 g/4 oz cherry tomatoes
75 g/3 oz black olives

For the anchovy dressing:

50 g can anchovy fillets
1 tsp Dijon mustard
1 small garlic clove, peeled and crushed
4 tbsp olive oil
1 tbsp lemon juice
freshly ground black pepper

For the ciabatta croûtons:

2 thick slices ciabatta bread
2 tbsp olive oil

1 Divide the endive and chicory into leaves and reserve some of the larger ones. Arrange the smaller leaves in a wide salad bowl.

2 Cut the fennel bulb in half from the stalk to the root end, then cut across in fine slices. Quarter the artichokes, then quarter and slice the cucumber and halve the tomatoes. Add to the salad bowl with the olives.

3 To make the dressing, drain the anchovies and put in a blender with the mustard, garlic, olive oil, lemon juice, 2 tablespoons of hot water and black pepper. Whiz together until smooth and thickened.

4 To make the croûtons, cut the bread into 1 cm/½ inch cubes. Heat the oil in a frying pan, add the bread cubes and fry for 3 minutes, turning frequently until golden. Remove and drain on absorbent kitchen paper.

5 Drizzle half the anchovy dressing over the prepared salad and toss to coat. Arrange the reserved endive and chicory leaves around the edge, then drizzle over the remaining dressing. Scatter over the croûtons and serve immediately.

Mushroom & Red Wine Pâté

Ingredients
Serves 4

3 large slices of
  white bread,
  crusts removed
2 tsp oil
1 small onion, peeled
  and finely chopped
1 garlic clove, peeled
  and crushed
350 g/12 oz button
  mushrooms, wiped
  and finely chopped
150 ml/¼ pint red wine
½ tsp dried
  mixed herbs
1 tbsp freshly
  chopped parsley
salt and freshly ground
  black pepper
2 tbsp low fat
  cream cheese

To serve:

finely chopped
  cucumber
finely chopped tomato

1 Preheat the oven to 180°C/350°F/Gas Mark 4. Cut the bread in half diagonally. Place the bread triangles on a baking tray and cook for 10 minutes.

2 Remove from the oven and split each bread triangle in half to make 12 triangles and return to the oven until golden and crisp. Leave to cool on a wire rack.

3 Heat the oil in a saucepan and gently cook the onion and garlic until transparent.

4 Add the mushrooms and cook, stirring for 3–4 minutes or until the mushroom juices start to run.

5 Stir the wine and herbs into the mushroom mixture and bring to the boil. Reduce the heat and simmer uncovered until all the liquid is absorbed.

6 Remove from the heat and season to taste with salt and pepper. Leave to cool.

7 When cold, beat in the soft cream cheese and adjust the seasoning. Place in a small clean bowl and chill until required. Serve the toast triangles with the cucumber and tomato.

Pad Thai Noodles with Mushrooms

Ingredients
Serves 4

125 g/4 oz flat rice noodles or rice vermicelli

1 tbsp vegetable oil

2 garlic cloves, peeled and finely chopped

1 medium egg, lightly beaten

225 g/8 oz mixed mushrooms, including shiitake, oyster, field, brown and wild mushrooms

2 tbsp lemon juice

1½ tbsp Thai fish sauce

½ tsp sugar

½ tsp cayenne pepper

2 spring onions, trimmed and cut into 2.5 cm/1 inch pieces

50 g/2 oz fresh beansprouts

To garnish:

chopped roasted peanuts

freshly chopped coriander

CHEF'S TIP

For an aromatic alternative to this dish add a handful of chopped fresh basil leaves to the recipe in step 3.

1 Cook the noodles according to the packet instructions. Drain well and reserve.

2 Heat a wok or large frying pan. Add the oil and garlic. Fry until just golden. Add the egg and stir quickly to break it up.

3 Cook for a few seconds before adding the noodles and mushrooms. Scrape down the sides of the pan to ensure they mix with the egg and garlic.

4 Add the lemon juice, fish sauce, sugar, cayenne pepper, spring onions and half of the beansprouts, stirring quickly all the time.

5 Cook over a high heat for a further 2–3 minutes until everything is heated through.

6 Turn on to a serving plate. Top with the remaining beansprouts. Garnish with the chopped peanuts and coriander and serve immediately.

Pan-cooked Chicken with Thai Spices

Ingredients
Serves 4

4 kaffir lime leaves
5 cm/2 inch piece of
    root ginger, peeled
    and chopped
300 ml/½ pint chicken
    stock, boiling
4 x 175 g/6 oz
    chicken breasts
2 tsp groundnut oil
5 tbsp coconut milk
1 tbsp fish sauce
2 red chillies, deseeded
    and finely chopped
225 g/8 oz Thai
    jasmine rice
1 tbsp lime juice
3 tbsp freshly
    chopped coriander
salt and freshly ground
    black pepper

To garnish:

wedges of lime
freshly chopped
    coriander

CHEF'S TIP
If you have trouble finding
fresh kaffir lime leaves,
use dried instead. These
are sold in supermarkets.
If using dried, crumble
lightly and use as above.

1 Lightly bruise the kaffir lime leaves and put in a bowl with the chopped ginger. Pour over the chicken stock, cover and leave to infuse for 30 minutes.

2 Meanwhile, cut each chicken breast into two pieces. Heat the oil in a large, non-stick frying pan or flameproof casserole dish and brown the chicken pieces for 2–3 minutes on each side.

3 Strain the infused chicken stock into the pan. Half cover the pan with a lid and gently simmer for 10 minutes.

4 Stir in the coconut milk, fish sauce and chopped chillies. Simmer, uncovered for 5–6 minutes, or until the chicken is tender and cooked through and the sauce has reduced slightly.

5 Meanwhile, cook the rice in boiling salted water according to the packet instructions. Drain the rice thoroughly.

6 Stir the lime juice and chopped coriander into the sauce. Season to taste with salt and pepper. Serve the chicken and sauce on a bed of rice. Garnish with wedges of lime and freshly chopped coriander and serve immediately.

Prawn & Chilli Soup

Ingredients
Serves 4

2 spring
   onions, trimmed
225 g/8 oz whole raw
   tiger prawns
750 ml/1¼ pint
   fish stock
finely grated rind and
   juice of 1 lime
1 tbsp fish sauce
1 red chilli, deseeded
   and chopped
1 tbsp soy sauce
1 lemon grass stalk
2 tbsp rice vinegar
4 tbsp freshly
   chopped coriander

CHEF'S TIP
For a more substantial dish add some glass (mung bean) noodles at the same time as the prawns.

1 To make spring onion curls, finely shred the spring onions lengthways. Place in a bowl of iced cold water and reserve.

2 Remove the heads and shells from the prawns leaving the tails intact.

3 Split the prawns almost in two to form a butterfly shape and individually remove the black thread that runs down the back of each one.

4 In a large pan heat the stock with the lime rind and juice, fish sauce, chilli and soy sauce.

5 Bruise the lemon grass by crushing it along its length with a rolling pin, then add to the stock mixture.

6 When the stock mixture is boiling add the prawns and cook until they are pink.

7 Remove the lemon grass and add the rice vinegar and coriander.

8 Ladle into bowls and garnish with the spring onion curls. Serve immediately.

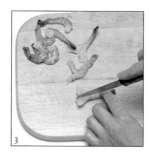

Ratatouille Mackerel

Ingredients
Serves 4

1 red pepper
1 tbsp olive oil
1 red onion, peeled
1 garlic clove, peeled
    and thinly sliced
2 courgettes, trimmed
    and cut into
    thick slices
400 g can of
    chopped tomatoes
sea salt and freshly
    ground black pepper
4 x 275 g/10 oz small
    mackerel, cleaned
    and heads removed
spray of olive oil
lemon juice
    for drizzling
12 fresh basil leaves
couscous or rice mixed
    with chopped
    parsley, to serve

1 Preheat the oven to 190°C/375°F/Gas Mark 5. Cut the top off the red pepper, remove the seeds and membrane, then cut into chunks. Cut the red onion into thick wedges.

2 Heat the oil in a large pan and cook the onion and garlic for 5 minutes or until beginning to soften.

3 Add the pepper chunks and courgette slices and cook for a further 5 minutes.

4 Pour in the chopped tomatoes with their juice and cook for a further 5 minutes. Season to taste with salt and pepper and pour into an ovenproof dish.

5 Season the fish with salt and pepper and arrange on top of the vegetables. Spray with a little olive oil and lemon juice. Cover and cook in the preheated oven for 20 minutes.

6 Remove the cover, add the basil leaves and return to the oven for a further 5 minutes. Serve immediately with couscous or rice mixed with parsley.

CHEF'S TIP
For an extra kick, add a little chopped, fresh chilli to the ratatouille.

Roasted Red Pepper, Tomato & Red Onion Soup

Ingredients
Serves 4

fine spray of oil
2 large red peppers,
   deseeded and
   roughly chopped
1 red onion, peeled and
   roughly chopped
350 g/12 oz
   tomatoes, halved
1 small crusty
   French loaf
1 garlic clove, peeled
600 ml/1 pint
   vegetable stock
salt and freshly ground
   black pepper
1 tsp Worcestershire
   sauce
4 tbsp half-fat
   fromage frais

1 Preheat the oven to 190°C/375°F/Gas Mark 5. Spray a large roasting tin with the oil and place the peppers and onion in the base. Cook in the oven for 10 minutes. Add the tomatoes and cook for a further 20 minutes or until the peppers are soft.

2 Cut the bread into 1 cm/½ inch slices. Cut the garlic clove in half and rub the cut edge of the garlic over the bread.

3 Place all the bread slices on a large baking tray, and bake in the preheated oven for 10 minutes, turning halfway through, until golden and crisp.

4 Remove the vegetables from the oven and allow to cool slightly, then blend in a food processor until smooth. Strain the vegetable mixture through a large nylon sieve into a saucepan, to remove the seeds and skin. Add the stock, season to taste with salt and pepper and stir to mix. Heat the soup gently until piping hot.

5 In a small bowl beat together the Worcestershire sauce with the fromage frais.

6 Pour the soup into warmed bowls and swirl a spoonful of the fromage frais mixture into each bowl. Serve immediately with the garlic toasts.

Sardines with Redcurrants

Ingredients

Serves 4

2 tbsp redcurrant jelly
finely grated rind
   of 1 lime
2 tbsp medium
   dry sherry
450 g /1 lb fresh
   sardines, cleaned and
   heads removed
sea salt and freshly
   ground black pepper
lime wedges,
   to garnish

To serve:

fresh redcurrants
fresh green salad

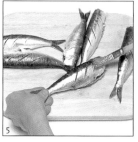

1 Preheat the grill and line the grill rack with tinfoil 2–3 minutes before cooking.

2 Warm the redcurrant jelly in a bowl standing over a pan of gently simmering water and stir until smooth. Add the lime rind and sherry to the bowl and stir well until blended.

3 Lightly rinse the sardines and pat dry with absorbent kitchen paper.

4 Place on a chopping board and with a sharp knife make several diagonal cuts across the flesh of each fish. Season the sardines inside the cavities with salt and pepper.

5 Gently brush the warm marinade over the skin and inside the cavities of the sardines.

6 Place on the grill rack and cook under the preheated grill for 8–10 minutes, or until the fish are cooked.

7 Carefully turn the sardines over at least once during grilling. Baste occasionally with the remaining redcurrant and lime marinade. Garnish with the redcurrants. Serve immediately with the salad and lime wedges.

Seared Pancetta-wrapped Cod

Ingredients

Serves 4

4 x 175 g/6 oz thick
   cod fillets
4 very thin slices
   of pancetta
3 tbsp capers
   in vinegar
1 tbsp of vegetable
   or sunflower oil
2 tbsp lemon juice
1 tbsp olive oil
freshly ground
   black pepper
1 tbsp freshly chopped
   parsley, to garnish

To serve:

freshly cooked
   vegetables
new potatoes

CHEF'S TIP

For a variation on this recipe, you could use salmon fillets in place of the cod.

1 Wipe the cod fillets and wrap each one with the pancetta. Secure each fillet with a cocktail stick and reserve.

2 Drain the capers and soak in cold water for 10 minutes to remove any excess salt, then drain and reserve.

3 Heat the oil in a large frying pan and sear the wrapped pieces of cod fillet for about 3 minutes on each side, turning carefully with a fish slice so as not to break up the fish.

4 Lower the heat then continue to cook for 2–3 minutes or until the fish is cooked thoroughly.

5 Meanwhile, place the reserved capers, lemon juice and olive oil into a small saucepan. Grind over the black pepper.

6 Place the saucepan over a low heat and bring to a gentle simmer, stirring continuously for 2–3 minutes.

7 Once the fish is cooked, garnish with the parsley and serve with the warm caper dressing, freshly cooked vegetables and new potatoes.

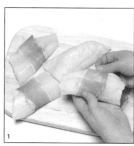

Seared Scallop Salad

Ingredients
Serves 4

12 king (large) scallops
1 tbsp low-fat spread
   or butter
2 tbsp orange juice
2 tbsp balsamic
   vinegar
1 tbsp clear honey
2 ripe pears, washed
125 g/4 oz rocket
125 g/4 oz watercress
50 g/2 oz walnuts
freshly ground
   black pepper

1 Clean the scallops removing the thin black vein from around the white meat and coral. Rinse thoroughly and dry on absorbent kitchen paper.

2 Cut into 2–3 thick slices, depending on the scallop size.

3 Heat a griddle pan or heavy-based frying pan, then when hot, add the low-fat spread or butter and allow to melt.

4 Once melted, sear the scallops for 1 minute on each side or until golden. Remove from the pan and reserve.

5 Briskly whisk together the orange juice, balsamic vinegar and honey to make the dressing and reserve.

6 With a small, sharp knife carefully cut the pears into quarters, core then cut into chunks.

7 Mix the rocket leaves, watercress, pear chunks and walnuts. Pile on to serving plates and top with the scallops.

8 Drizzle over the dressing and grind over plenty of black pepper. Serve immediately.

CHEF'S TIP
It is worth remembering that oysters are in season between September and March, when they will not only be at their best, but they may also be slightly cheaper in price.

Seared Tuna with Pernod & Thyme

Ingredients

Serves 4

4 tuna or
   swordfish steaks
salt and freshly ground
   black pepper
3 tbsp Pernod
1 tbsp olive oil
zest and juice of 1 lime
2 tsp fresh
   thyme leaves
4 sundried tomatoes

To serve:

freshly cooked
   mixed rice
tossed green salad

1 Wipe the fish steaks with a damp cloth or dampened kitchen paper.

2 Season both sides of the fish with salt and pepper, then place in a shallow bowl and reserve.

3 Mix together the Pernod, olive oil, lime zest and juice with the fresh thyme leaves.

4 Finely chop the sundried tomatoes and add to the Pernod mixture.

5 Pour the Pernod mixture over the fish and chill in the refrigerator for about 2 hours, spooning the marinade occasionally over the fish.

6 Heat a griddle or heavy-based frying pan. Drain the fish, reserving the marinade. Cook the fish for 3–4 minutes on each side for a steak that is still slightly pink in the middle. Or, cook the fish for 1–2 minutes longer on each side if you prefer your fish cooked through.

7 Place the remaining marinade in a small saucepan and bring to the boil. Pour the marinade over the fish and serve immediately, with the mixed rice and salad.

Spicy Chicken Skewers with Mango Tabbouleh

Ingredients

Serves 4

400 g/14 oz chicken breast fillet
200 ml/7 fl oz natural low fat yogurt
1 garlic clove, peeled and crushed
1 small red chilli, deseeded and finely chopped
½ tsp ground turmeric
finely grated rind and juice of ½ lemon
sprigs of fresh mint, to garnish

For the mango tabbouleh:

175 g/6 oz bulgur wheat
1 tsp olive oil
juice of ½ lemon
½ red onion, finely chopped
1 ripe mango, halved, stoned, peeled and chopped
¼ cucumber, finely diced
2 tbsp freshly chopped parsley
2 tbsp freshly shredded mint
salt and finely ground black pepper

1 If using wooden skewers, pre-soak them in cold water for at least 30 minutes. This stops them from burning during grilling.

2 Cut the chicken into 5 x 1 cm/2 x ½ inch strips and place in a shallow dish.

3 Mix together the yogurt, garlic, chilli, turmeric, lemon rind and juice. Pour over the chicken and toss to coat. Cover and leave to marinate in the refrigerator for up to 8 hours.

4 To make the tabbouleh, put the bulgur wheat in a bowl. Pour over enough boiling water to cover. Put a plate over the bowl. Leave to soak for 20 minutes.

5 Whisk together the oil and lemon juice in a bowl. Add the red onion and leave to marinade for 10 minutes.

6 Drain the bulgur wheat and squeeze out any excess moisture in a clean tea towel. Add to the red onion with the mango, cucumber, herbs and season to taste with salt and pepper. Toss together.

7 Thread the chicken strips on to eight wooden or metal skewers. Cook under a hot grill for 8 minutes. Turn and brush with the marinade, until the chicken is lightly browned and cooked through.

8 Spoon the tabbouleh on to individual plates. Arrange the chicken skewers on top and garnish with the sprigs of mint. Serve warm or cold.

Sticky-glazed Spatchcocked Poussins

Ingredients
Serves 4

2 poussins, each about
    700 g/1½ lb
salt and freshly ground
    black pepper
4 kumquats,
    thinly sliced
assorted salad leaves,
    crusty bread or new
    potatoes,to serve

For the glaze:

zest of 1 small lemon,
    finely grated
1 tbsp lemon juice
1 tbsp dry sherry
2 tbsp clear honey
2 tbsp dark soy sauce
2 tbsp whole-grain
    mustard
1 tsp tomato purée
½ tsp Chinese five
    spice powder

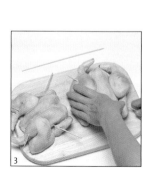

1 Preheat the grill just before cooking. Place one of the poussins breast-side down on a board. Using poultry shears, cut down one side of the backbone. Cut down the other side of the backbone. Remove the bone.

2 Open out the poussin and press down hard on the breast bone with the heel of your hand to break it and to flatten the poussin.

3 Thread two skewers crosswise through the bird to keep it flat, ensuring that each skewer goes through a wing and out through the leg on the opposite side. Repeat with the other bird. Season both sides of the bird with salt and pepper.

4 To make the glaze, mix together the lemon zest and juice, sherry, honey, soy sauce, mustard, tomato purée and Chinese five spice powder and use to brush all over the poussins.

5 Place the poussins skin-side down on a grill rack and grill under a medium heat for 15 minutes, brushing halfway through with more glaze.

6 Turn the poussins over and grill for 10 minutes. Brush again with glaze and arrange the kumquat slices on top. Grill for a further 15 minutes until well-browned and cooked through. If they start to brown too quickly, turn down the grill a little.

7 Remove the skewers and cut each poussin in half along the breastbone. Serve with the salad, crusty bread or new potatoes.

Teriyaki Beef

Ingredients

Serves 4

550 g/1¼ lb rump or
  sirloin steak
1 medium onion, peeled
  and finely sliced
5 cm/2 inch piece of
  fresh root ginger,
  peeled and
  coarsely chopped
1 bird's-eye chilli,
  deseeded and
  finely chopped
6 tbsp light soy sauce
2 tbsp sake or
  sweet sherry
1 tbsp lemon juice
1 tsp clear honey
250 g/9 oz
  glutinous rice
sunflower oil,
  for spraying

To garnish:

carrot matchsticks
daikon matchsticks
sprigs of
  fresh coriander

CHEF'S TIP
Bird's-eye chillies are
extremely hot. If you
prefer a milder taste use
one of the larger varieties
of chilli. The larger
varieties contain less of
the volatile oil that gives
chillies their fiery taste.

1 Trim the steak, discarding any fat or gristle, and place in a non-metallic shallow dish. Scatter the sliced onion over the steak. Mix the ginger with the chilli and sprinkle over the steak and onion.

2 Blend the soy sauce with the sake or sherry, the lemon juice and honey. Stir well, then pour over the steak and onion. Cover and leave to marinate in the refrigerator for at least 1 hour, longer if time permits. Turn the steak over, or occasionally spoon the marinade over the meat, during this time.

3 Place the rice in a saucepan with 450 ml/¾ pint of water and cook for 15 minutes, or until tender. Drain if necessary, then pack into four warmed, oiled individual moulds. Quickly invert onto four individual warm plates and keep warm.

4 Spray or brush a griddle pan with oil, then heat until really hot. Drain the steak and cook in the griddle pan for 2–3 minutes on each side, or until cooked to personal preference. Remove from the pan and slice thinly. Arrange on the warm serving plates, garnish with the carrot and daikon matchsticks and coriander sprigs, then serve.

Tuna Chowder

Ingredients
Serves 4

2 tsp oil
1 onion, peeled and
  finely chopped
2 sticks of celery,
  trimmed and
  finely sliced
1 tbsp plain flour
600 ml/1 pint
  skimmed milk
200 g can tuna
  in water
320 g can sweetcorn
  in water, drained
2 tsp freshly
  chopped thyme
salt and freshly ground
  black pepper
pinch cayenne pepper
2 tbsp freshly
  chopped parsley

1 Heat the oil in a large, heavy-based saucepan. Add the onion and celery and gently cook for about 5 minutes, stirring from time to time until the onion is softened.

2 Stir in the flour and cook for about 1 minute to thicken.

3 Draw the pan off the heat and gradually pour in the milk, stirring throughout.

4 Add the tuna and its liquid, the drained sweetcorn and the thyme.

5 Mix gently, then bring to the boil. Cover and simmer for 5 minutes.

6 Remove the pan from the heat and season to taste with salt and pepper.

7 Sprinkle the chowder with the cayenne pepper and chopped parsley. Divide into soup bowls and serve immediately.

CHEF'S TIP
This creamy soup works equally well with equivalent amounts of crab meat, instead of the tuna.

Turkey & Tomato Tagine

Ingredients

Serves 4

For the meatballs:

450 g/1 lb fresh
   turkey mince
1 small onion,
   peeled and very
   finely chopped
1 garlic clove, peeled
   and crushed
1 tbsp freshly
   chopped coriander
1 tsp ground cumin
1 tbsp olive oil
salt and freshly
   ground black pepper

For the sauce:

1 onion, peeled and
   finely chopped
1 garlic clove, peeled
   and crushed
150 ml/¼ pint
   turkey stock
400 g can of
   chopped tomatoes
½ tsp ground cumin
½ tsp ground
   cinnamon
pinch of
   cayenne pepper
freshly chopped parsley
freshly chopped herbs,
   to garnish
freshly cooked couscous
   or rice, to serve

1 Preheat the oven to 190°C/375°F/Gas Mark 5. Put all the ingredients for the meatballs in a bowl, except the oil and mix well. Season to taste with salt and pepper. Shape into 20 balls, about the size of walnuts.

2 Put on a tray, cover lightly and chill in the refrigerator while making the sauce.

3 Put the onion and garlic in a pan with 125 ml/4 fl oz of the stock. Cook over a low heat until all the stock has evaporated. Continue cooking for 1 minute, or until the onions begin to colour.

4 Add the remaining stock to the pan with the tomatoes, cumin, cinnamon and cayenne pepper. Simmer for 10 minutes, until slightly thickened and reduced. Stir in the parsley and season to taste.

5 Heat the oil in a large non-stick frying pan and cook the meatballs in two batches until lightly browned all over.

6 Lift the meatballs out with a slotted spoon and drain on kitchen paper.

7 Pour the sauce into a tagine or an ovenproof casserole. Top with the meatballs, cover and cook in the preheated oven for 25–30 minutes, or until the meatballs are cooked through and the sauce is bubbling. Garnish with freshly chopped herbs and serve immediately on a bed of couscous or plain boiled rice.

Wild Garlic Mushrooms with Pizza Breadsticks

Ingredients
Serves 6

For the breadsticks:

7 g/1/4 oz dried yeast
250 ml/8 fl oz
    warm water
400 g/14 oz strong,
    plain flour
2 tbsp olive oil
1 tsp salt

9 tbsp olive oil
4 garlic cloves, peeled
    and crushed
450 g/1 lb mixed wild
    mushrooms, wiped
    and dried
salt and freshly ground
    black pepper
1 tbsp freshly
    chopped parsley
1 tbsp freshly
    chopped basil
1 tsp fresh
    oregano leaves
juice of 1 lemon

1 Preheat oven to 240°C/475°F/Gas Mark 9, 15 minutes before baking. Place the dried yeast in the warm water for 10 minutes. Place the flour in a large bowl and gradually blend in the olive oil, salt and the dissolved yeast.

2 Knead on a lightly floured surface to form a smooth and pliable dough. Cover with clingfilm and leave in a warm place for 15 minutes to allow the dough to rise, then roll out again and cut into sticks of equal length. Cover and leave to rise again for 10 minutes. Brush with the olive oil, sprinkle with salt and bake in the preheated oven for 10 minutes.

3 Pour 3 tablespoons of the oil into a frying pan and add the crushed garlic. Cook over a very low heat, stirring well for 3–4 minutes to flavour the oil.

4 Cut the wild mushrooms into bite-sized slices if very large, then add to the pan. Season well with salt and pepper and cook very gently for 6–8 minutes, or until tender.

5 Whisk the fresh herbs, the remaining olive oil and lemon juice together. Pour over the mushrooms and heat through. Season to taste and place on individual serving dishes. Serve with the pizza breadsticks.

Zesty Whole-baked Fish

Ingredients
Serves 8

1.8 kg/4 lb whole
   salmon, cleaned
sea salt and freshly
   ground black pepper
50 g/2 oz low fat spread
1 garlic clove, peeled
   and finely sliced
zest and juice of 1 lemon
zest of 1 orange
1 tsp freshly
   grated nutmeg
3 tbsp Dijon mustard
2 tbsp fresh
   white breadcrumbs
2 bunches fresh dill
1 bunch fresh tarragon
1 lime sliced
150 ml/¼ pint half-fat
   crème fraîche
450 ml/¾ pint
   fromage frais
dill sprigs, to garnish

1 Preheat the oven to 220°C/425°F/Gas Mark 7. Lightly rinse the fish and pat dry with absorbent kitchen paper. Season the cavity with a little salt and pepper. Make several diagonal cuts across the flesh of the fish and season.

2 Mix together the low fat spread, garlic, lemon and orange zest and juice, nutmeg, mustard and fresh breadcrumbs. Mix well together. Spoon the breadcrumb mixture into the slits with a small sprig of dill. Place the remaining herbs inside the fish cavity. Weigh the fish and calculate the cooking time. Allow 10 minutes per 450 g/1 lb.

3 Lay the fish on a double thickness tinfoil. If liked, smear the fish with a little low fat spread. Top with the lime slices and fold the foil into a parcel. Chill in the refrigerator for about 15 minutes.

4 Place in a roasting tin and cook in the preheated oven for the calculated cooking time. Fifteen minutes before the end of cooking, open the foil and return until the skin begins to crisp. Remove the fish from the oven and stand for 10 minutes.

5 Pour the juices from the roasting tin into a saucepan. Bring to the boil and stir in the crème fraîche and fromage frais. Simmer for 3 minutes or until hot. Garnish with dill sprigs and serve immediately.

Index